AF279199

SPIES

Written by Paul Stevenson

CONTENTS

First published in 2026 by
Hungry Tomato Ltd
F15, Old Bakery Studios, Blewetts Wharf, Malpas Road,
Truro, Cornwall, TR1 1QH, UK.

Thanks to our editor, Julie Tofflemire.

A CIP catalog record for this book is available from the
British Library.

ISBN 9781835694459

Manufactured in the USA

Discover more at
www.hungrytomato.com

DISCLAIMER:
Spies often operate outside of the law, and they take many risks. Leave the spying to the professionals!
All words in **BOLD** can be found in the glossary.

TOP SECRET

Step into the world of spies with daring missions, clever disguises, and high-tech gadgets.

One of the most famous spies of all time was James Bond. He was created in the 1950s by the novelist Ian Fleming.

Bond, also known as 007, is a fictional character, appearing in 12 original novels and over 25 films.

But spies aren't just in books or on the movie screens. They are at work behind the scenes all the time. What information are they after... and how will they uncover it?

GADGETS AND GIZMOS

The equipment used by spies is never what it seems...

Something may look like an everyday object at first glance. But on closer inspection, it turns out to have a secret function!

Spies can make secret video recordings with tiny cameras. They may be **concealed** almost anywhere, including in pens, watches, and even buttons!

Coins, books, golf balls, and more have been designed with hidden compartments for secret items.

During the Second World War, some British agents were armed with hairbrushes! Although they looked ordinary, these brushes had a secret drawer for hiding maps and photographs.

Surveillance camera

SECRET WEAPONS

Everyday things can also be adapted to hide weapons.

In 1978, a Bulgarian writer named Georgi Markov was murdered in London, UK by a foreign spy.

He was killed by a tiny **pellet** of poison that was jabbed into his leg using the tip of a deadly umbrella.

The "Kiss of Death" was a pistol that could only fire one shot, but it was small enough to hide inside a lipstick holder.

"Kiss of Death" lipstick pistol

Dropping poison into someone's drink could mean the end to an enemy. No one would suspect a ring, right?

It looks like a normal ring. But poison can be hidden inside.

DISGUISED DOCUMENTS

Spies work hard to get their information, so they don't want it to get into the wrong hands!

During the Second World War, German spies sent secret documents to each other by shrinking them to 1/400th of their original size.

Known as microdots, they could be as small as the period at the end of this sentence. Their tiny size made them easy to hide.

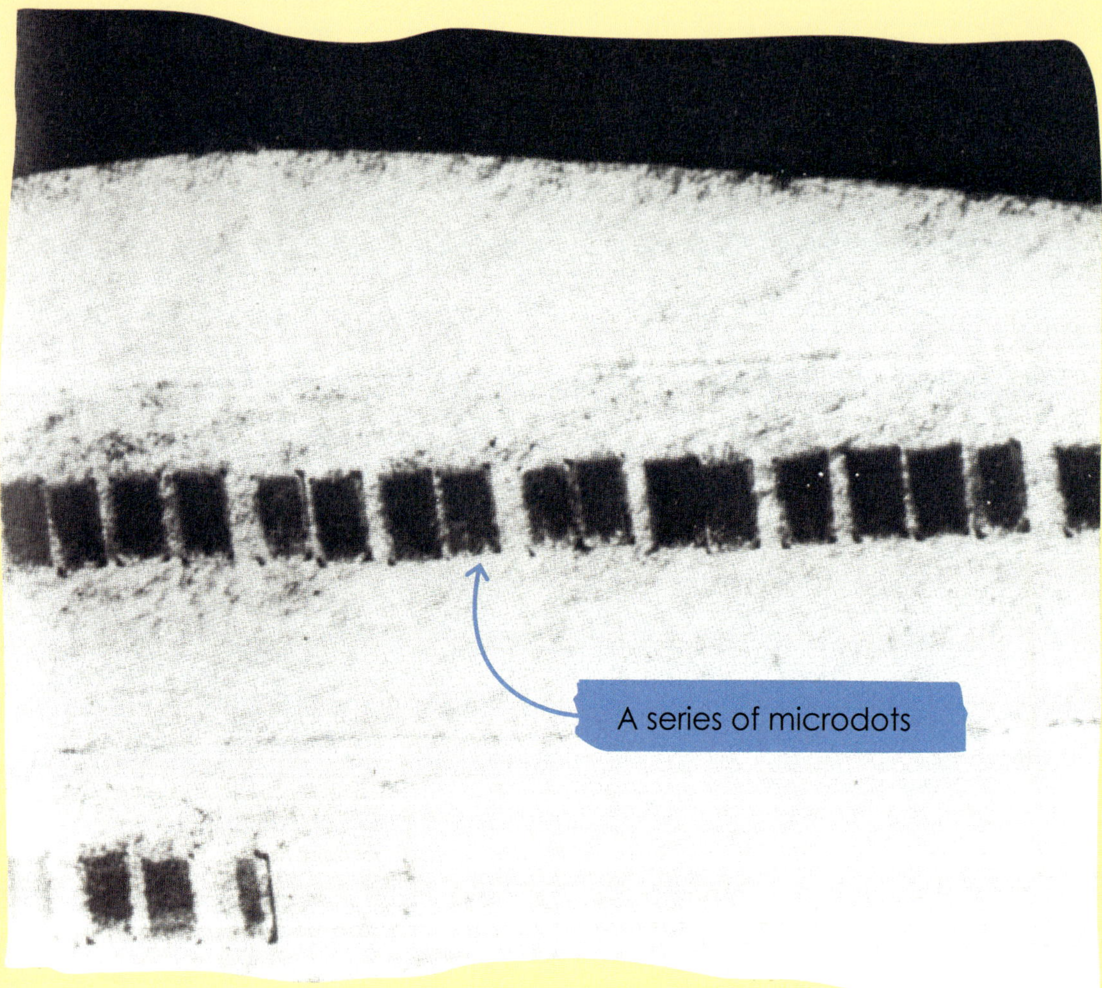

DO YOU WANT TO TRY WRITING YOUR OWN SECRET MESSAGE WITH INVISIBLE INK?

Dip a cotton bud or paintbrush in fresh lemon juice and write your message on a blank piece of paper. When the juice dries, your message will disappear.

To reveal the message, get a grown-up to help you add heat! They can iron the paper, warm it with a hairdryer, or hold it close to an **incandescent** light bulb.

DEAD DROP

Meeting in person with another spy can be risky. So, spies have found other ways to pass items back and forth.

A dead drop, or dead letter box (DLB), is a place where spies can secretly leave messages and items for each other to collect.

In the 1980s, the KGB (the former Soviet Union's secret spy organization) used a marble column in a London church as a DLB.

A small blue chalk mark on a nearby lamppost showed agents that a message was waiting to be collected.

Dead drop locations are usually common items, like under a stone, behind a loose brick, or in an unused mailbox.

Sometimes, documents or other items are placed in a dead drop spike. The container is resistant to water and can be stuck into the ground or placed in shallow water.

A dead drop spike

REAL SPIES

The best spies in the world are probably the ones we've never heard of – their secret identity is still safe!

Sidney Reilly (1873-1925), known as the "Ace of Spies", was a Russian-born secret agent who worked for the British government. He gathered information on oil developments, railroad progress, naval activities, and more.

Author Ian Fleming based the character James Bond on Reilly!

One of the most famous female spies was a dancer known as "Mata Hari" (1876-1917). During the First World War, she gathered useful information from her many admirers and then secretly passed it on to the German Secret Service.

Many important people came to see her show. But secretly, Mata Hari was watching them just as closely as they were watching her!

EYE IN THE SKY

The latest spy planes, drones, and satellites give secret agents an amazing bird's-eye view.

The B-21 Raider's unique shape makes it difficult for advanced **radar** systems to spot. It also has a special **coating** that absorbs radar waves rather than reflecting them.

With these and other features, it can sneak into enemy territory!

A military UAV

A UAV, unmanned aerial vehicle, can gather information from the skies. The pilot can operate the aircraft **remotely** and stay hidden far away!

Top-secret spy satellites can **detect** the launch of missiles and provide an early warning of an enemy attack.

They can also track the movement of soldiers, ships, and tanks – and beam photographs of them back down to Earth.

A satellite in orbit

CODE-CRACKER

Spies use secret codes when sending messages. This way, even if enemies get hold of the message, they won't be able to work out what it means.

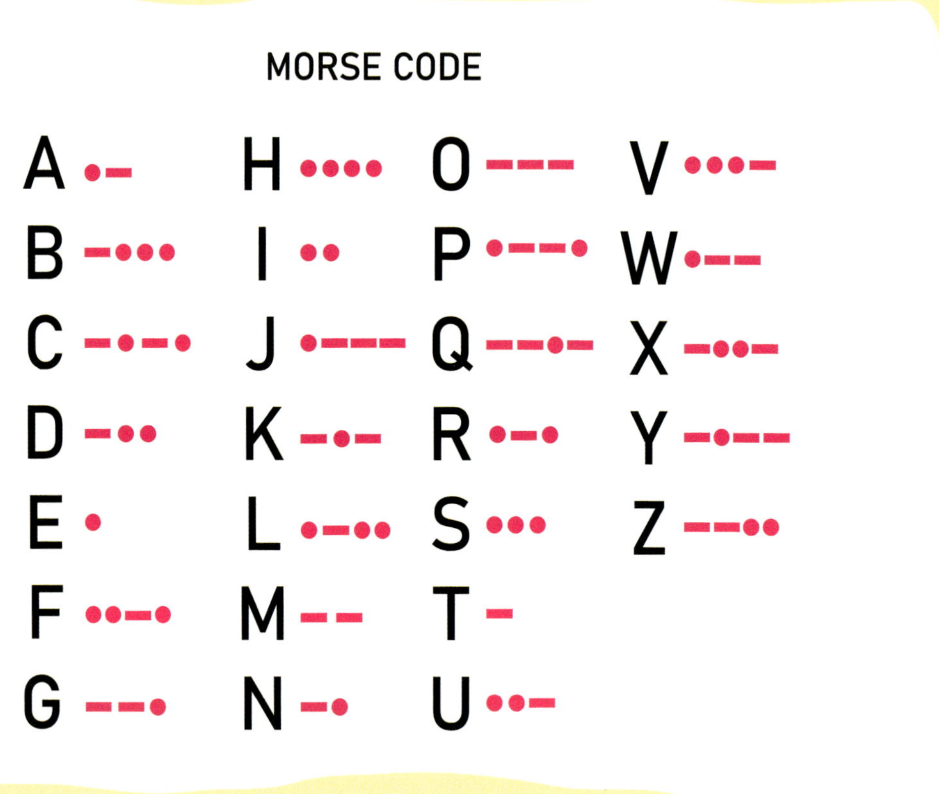

Morse code, invented in 1840 by Samuel Morse, was used to send messages by **telegraph**. Each letter of the alphabet is represented by a series of dots and dashes.

This code, and others, were used by spies in unique ways. They could broadcast the code using flashing lights or even knitted into clothing!

During the Second World War, German spies sent secret messages using a code called Enigma. To put a message into code, they used a special keyboard.

What the Germans didn't realise was that a team of Polish mathematicians had cracked the code a year before the war started!

SPY LINGO

If you really want to keep up in the world of spying, you'll have to learn some of the words spies use...

DOUBLE AGENT

A double agent is a spy who has secretly changed sides. Their old friends still think they are **loyal** when, in fact, they are passing on secrets to the enemy!

A MOLE

A mole is someone who is planted in an enemy organization to gain access to secret information.

SLEEPER AGENT

A sleeper agent is sent to live in an enemy country and pretend to be a normal citizen. The agent isn't "activated" until much, much later - this is when their spying begins!

A BUG

A bug is a hidden microphone used for listening in on other people's conversations. They are tiny – even as small as a grain of rice!

SPY AGENCIES

Governments around the world have their own intelligence agencies. Of course, these are only the ones we're allowed to know about!

Agencies like the FBI (Federal Bureau of Investigation) and MI5 (the Security Service) focus on **domestic** crimes.

They also engage in counterintelligence – stopping spies from other countries discovering their secrets.

The CIA (Central Intelligence Agency) in the USA and MI6 (the Secret Intelligence Service) in the UK handle international **espionage.**

They perform **covert** operations to gather information outside of their home country.

Agencies such as Mossad (Israel), the FSB (Russia, the successor of the KGB), and others perform similar functions.

Sometimes, police forces in different countries work together. The International Criminal Police Organization ("Interpol") enables them to share information.

GOING DIGITAL

Crime is getting smarter, and so are the spies! As technology evolves, secret agents need to use the most modern methods to stay one step ahead.

Hackers can use the Internet to gain access to **servers** and computers.

Their targets may include military data, trade secrets, new technologies, and political plans.

To combat this, some governments and companies hire "white hat hackers". These hackers are given permission to try to hack into a system. This helps to show where the weaknesses are.

An air-gapped network is a special kind of computer network that is completely cut off from the Internet, Wi-Fi, and other outside connections.

Since it doesn't connect to the internet, it helps keep important information extra safe from hackers and other online dangers.

WOULD I LIE TO YOU?

Spies need accurate information. Can a machine really tell the difference between the truth and a lie?

Polygraphs, commonly known as "lie detectors", were invented in 1921.

They measure tiny changes in a suspect's **blood pressure,** heartbeat, and breathing while the person answers questions. The results appear on a graph.

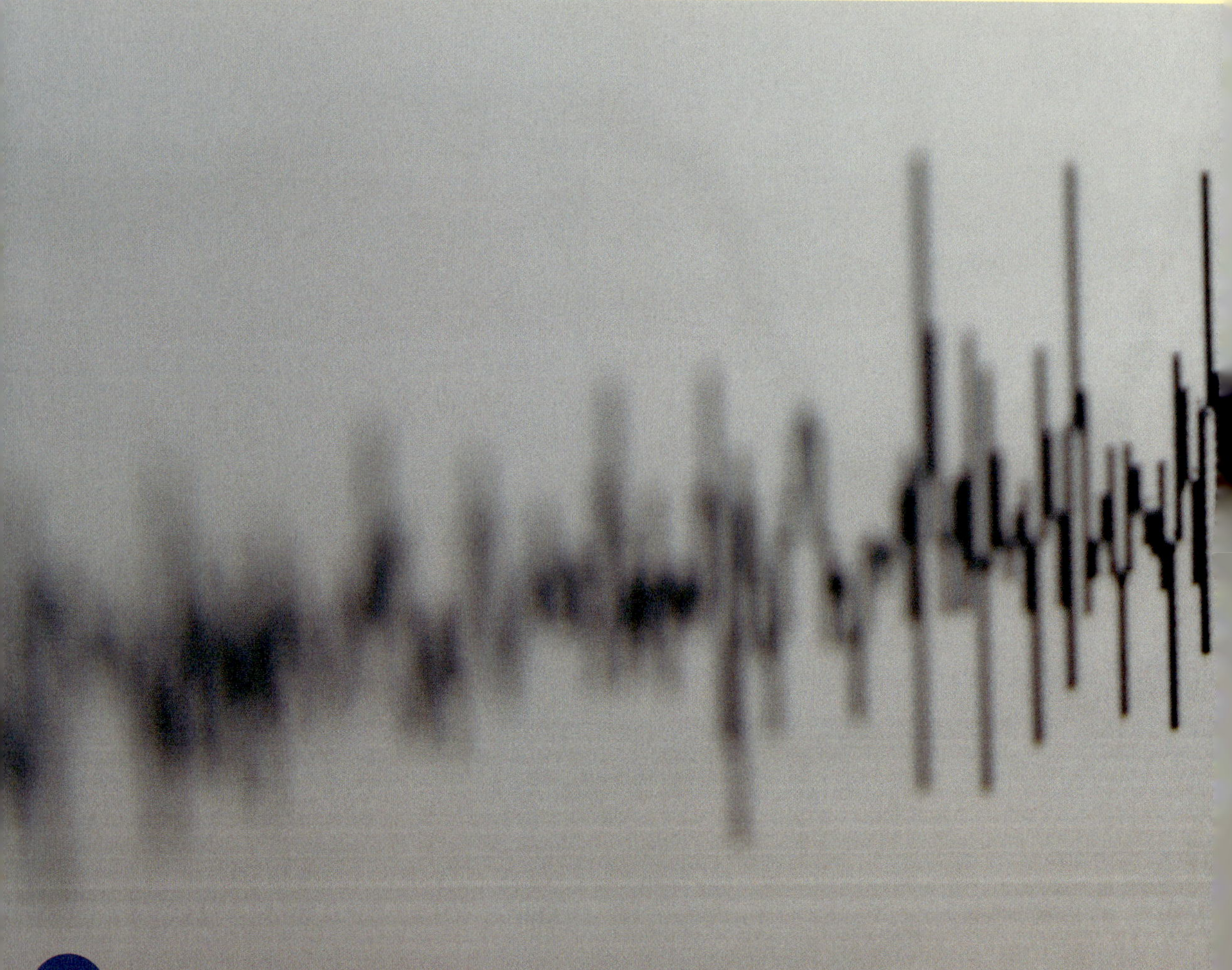

This information can be used as a guide to tell whether or not the person is telling the truth. However, the **accuracy** of polygraph tests has been debated.

Some people use strategies to beat the test. For example, they tell small lies during the control questions, the ones used to get a **baseline** of the person's behavior.

Peson being tested on a polygraph machine

MASTER OF DISGUISE

If you want to be a spy, you must learn how to keep your real identity a secret and observe people without them noticing who you are.

Sometimes just blending in is the best disguise, so spies wear everyday clothes. An eye-catching outfit would only attract attention!

In the earlier days, a newspaper gave people something to pretend to read while they were secretly watching something (or someone) else.

Today, you're probably better off pretending to be on your phone.

Spies can also change the look of their face by using **prosthetics**, like a fake nose or bald cap, and makeup.

Unfortunately, the mask peel-off scenes you see in movies like *Mission Impossible* and *Black Widow* are movie tricks rather than real spy tech!

Applying a bald cap

HOW TO BECOME A SPY!

Are you ready to join the world of espionage? An intelligence officer isn't quite 007, but here's what you need to know.

- Most government agencies require a university degree, so keep studying!
- You'll need great teamwork, analytical, and communication skills.
- Honesty is essential, as you'll be trusted with **sensitive** information.
- You'll have to pass a thorough background check of your finances, work history, travel, and ties to foreign countries. They'll even talk to your family and friends!

GLOSSARY

accuracy – the state of being correct and exact.

baseline – a standard of what is "normal" to use for comparison.

blood pressure – the force of one's blood pushing against the walls of blood vessels as it moves through the body.

coating – a thin layer of something covering a surface.

concealed – hidden.

covert – secret or hidden.

detect – to notice or discover something.

domestic – within a country; the opposite of international.

espionage – the activity of spying or secretly getting information.

HQ – headquarters, the center of an organization. This is where spy training and mission planning happens.

incandescent – an incandescent light bulb makes light by heating a wire; LEDs are not incandescent.

intelligence officer – a person working for a government who collects and analyzes information about other organizations and countries.

loyal – staying faithful to a person, group, or organization.

pellet – a small, round piece of material.

prosthetics – artificial (not real) body parts.

radar – a machine that uses radio waves to sense objects and natural structures like clouds.

remotely – done or performed from a distance, not in person.

sensitive – containing private information that should not be shared.

servers – computer systems that provide data and services on a network.

telegraph – an old-fashioned machine that sent messages using electrical signals.

INDEX

Picture credits:
(t=top; b=bottom; m=middle; l=left; r=right):
Shutterstock: Allycreations 26-27bg; Andrei Armiagov 17br; Andrey_Popev 30mr; APChanel 5bg; Art_Pictures 9bl, 9br; b.asia 6-7bg; BreizhAtao 23tr; DC Studio 30b; Deepadesigns 1bg; Goir 4b; Golden Dayz 25t; Jeremy Walter 8b; Kavi designs 18m; Maradek 16br; Metamorworks 14b; Nejron Photo 29b; Ollyy 28b; Razoomanet 2-3bg; Salah Ait Mokhtar 23tl; Standret 27mr; Stefano carciccio 24b; Svet foto 22ml; T.N. Sursock 12-13bg; Wita Design 11bg; Yevhen Prozhyrko 6bl; Zenitx 19b; Zephyr_p 20-21bg. Wikipedia: By Joyofmuseums - Own work, CC BY-SA 4.0, https://commons.wikimedia.org/w/index.php?curid=64714491 9t; By Unknown author - https://www.nsa.gov/Portals/70/documents/about/cryptologic-heritage/historical-figures-publications/publications/wwii/cryptologic_aspects_of_gi.pdf, Public Domain, https://commons.wikimedia.org/w/index.php?curid=32891795 10b; By The Central Intelligence Agency - "Dead" Drop Spike, Public Domain, https://commons.wikimedia.org/w/index.php?curid=29197364 13ml; Public Domain, https://commons.wikimedia.org/w/index.php?curid=79079010 14mr; Commons, Public Domain, https://commons.wikimedia.org/w/index.php?curid=19060418 23bm; By Ministère des Armées / Vector graphic : Futurhit12 - Own work, Public Domain, https://commons.wikimedia.org/w/index.php?curid=78186688 23br; By Ministry of State Security of the People's Republic of China - https://www.sgss8.net/tpdq/10521890/, Public Domain, https://commons.wikimedia.org/w/index.php?curid=132087854 23bl; By Gibson Torreon C - Own work, CC BY-SA 4.0, https://commons.wikimedia.org/w/index.php?curid=35549785 21ml; By Lt. Col. Leslie Pratt - MQ-9 Reaper UAV.jpg, Public Domain, https://commons.wikimedia.org/w/index.php?curid=68095681 17t; By USAF - https://www.dvidshub.net/image/8423170/b-21-raider-continues-flight-test-production, Public Domain, https://commons.wikimedia.org/w/index.php?curid=148631292 16m; By Unknown photographer - Biography Online, Public Domain, https://commons.wikimedia.org/w/index.php?curid=33028944 15b; By NVO - Own work, CC BY-SA 3.0, https://commons.wikimedia.org/w/index.php?curid=12624869 22mr.

Every effort has been made to trace the copyright holders, and we apologize in advance for any unintentional omissions. We would be pleased to insert the appropriate acknowledgments in any subsequent edition of this publication.